Chapter One - The Early Years

Mrs Emily Clapham opened her dressmaking salon in King
Hull in 1887 and by the 1890s was highly regarded as
dressmaker. Miss Emily MacVitie, as she was formerly known
Cheltenham in 1856 and left school at an early age to serve
apprenticeship at Marshall and Snelgrove in Scarborough. She
up pins from the floor and gained a thorough training in the dressmaking trade right through to the finished product. It was clear that she was incredibly talented and with her eye for fashion and colour, combined with sound business sense, she gave every indication that she would make a successful career out of dressmaking. Emily eventually went into business with her husband, Haigh Clapham and they invested their savings in the purchase of Number 1 Kingston Square, a yellow brick Victorian house in Hull.

From this address Emily Clapham set out to win the patronage of the well-to-do families of Hull and the East Riding. Kingston Square was a respectable Victorian residential area with large houses and impressive public buildings surrounding it. Her beginnings were humble and fabric for each order was purchased locally as and when it was needed. However, the premises were carefully designed to reflect the exclusivity and detail which would attract the high society ladies of the region. An early and important client was Miss Muriel Wilson of Tranby Croft.

Madame Clapham's skill was to select aspects of the latest Paris and London fashion-houses and put them together to create her own designs. Mannequins remember the names of Fremo, Hartnell, Molyneaux and Worth as some of the labels Madame Clapham used. Each season she purchased a selection of model gowns from these fashion houses and put together an outfit using a bodice from one dress, a sleeve from another, producing her own creation. She had a talent for selecting the right colour, cut, finish and trimmings to suit her client and create a very elegant and exquisite Madame Clapham dress.

Madame Clapham has been described as an imposing figure, dressed immaculately but always in black or navy. Her floor length dresses with trains, which she wore long after they were fashionable, rustled as she moved around the salon and she left behind the perfume of lavender which she wore. Emily was by all accounts a large woman with piercing blue eyes, rosy cheeks and an abundance of blonde hair worn on top of her head in an elaborate fashion. She was able to combine the skills of polite firmness towards her clients with running a very strict and disciplined regime in the workrooms. She was a strict Christian Scientist and helped her family out financially or by giving them employment. Her great niece Pat Walker remembers her, "Great Aunt Emmie, as I remember her, was a gracious lady with piled up golden hair. She had become a Christian Scientist. I think my mother may have been one of her favourites. When Madge married, Emmie's present to her was her wedding dress. Family history recalls that most of Haigh's generosity to his family was prompted by Emmie. It was, after all, her flair for fashion designing that had made him a wealthy man."

Eric Wall, son of Emily Wall recalls visiting his aunt, Madame Clapham, in her later years, at home in Cottingham, "Aunt Emmy, at her large house in South Street, became someone I visited with my mother many summer Saturday afternoons. They talked, presumably about business; I sat. On occasions my mother was given money for my school expenses. On perhaps the last of these occasions I remember Aunt Emmy giving my mother £1 (a huge sum of money in those days) and my saying thank you to Aunt Emmy through her ear trumpet. But then this process was followed by further one pound notes for each of which, much against my inclination, I had to say thank you." Despite her perceived severeness Madame Clapham demonstrated generosity to her family in this way.

These were the circumstances in which Emily Clapham started her dressmaking business from Kingston Square. From modest beginnings in 1887 the salon blossomed into a thriving and successful business, which earned itself a unique reputation in the region, expanding rapidly in the 1890s.

Chapter Two - The Heyday

Madame Clapham's reputation as a fine dressmaker was at its height from 1890 until the outbreak of the First World War. This was an era of strict dress codes which elegant ladies followed each day. There were many social engagements, including race meetings, balls, dinner parties and musical evenings, which required certain styles of dress, in exquisite fabrics. Locally, there were annual events such as the Hunt Ball or evenings of entertainment at the Assembly Rooms, which was on the opposite side of Kingston Square. The salon would be particularly busy leading up to Christmas, with an array of social festivities planned by prominent families. Madame Clapham also received many wedding orders, often creating the dresses for the bride and bridesmaids and even for some lady guests. Ladies increasingly looked to Madame Clapham for the latest seasonal offerings. For Spring-Summer 1902 the salon was promoting gowns in "soft clinging material such as voile, canvas, and a kind of woollen crepe-de-chine, mostly in delicate pastel colourings", to be trimmmed with all kinds of lace. Madame Clapham's range also appears to have expanded, offering a "variety of silk petticoats made to order to match gowns or the dainty corsets which are now procurable at this address." (1)

In the 1890s the salon was so successful that Madame Clapham purchased number two Kingston Square in 1891. In December 1901 Madame proclaimed, "I am always very busy". Dresses had just been completed for the forthcoming local Golf Ball. Madame Clapham talked of her plans for expansion to cope with demand, "I am having the showrooms enlarged and extensive alterations made during the next three months, also more workrooms added. I have now accommodation for 150 work people, but find the business increasing so much I must have more room." Number three Kingston Square was purchased just before the First World War, with a legacy left to Madame Clapham by her aunt. To keep up to date with changing styles, at the turn of the century Madame Clapham talked of visiting Paris three or four times each year on average. She also claimed that, "representatives of the best French houses come over periodically to wait upon me specially with their newest goods." (2)

Madame Clapham was so successful in attracting clients from beyond the East Riding that each season she would travel to York, Harrogate, Grimsby and London. In a hectic schedule, ladies would make appointments with Madame at the Royal Station Hotels and Mandeville Hotel in London to view examples of the latest creations. Visits were also made to Sandringham to display garments to Queen Maud of Norway, Madame Clapham's most esteemed client. At the first fitting, exact measurements of their figures were taken in order to create a dummy, cut out of seven pieces of leno, which was a stiff cotton gauze. This allowed outfits to be accurately made in Hull for clients who could not attend the salon in person. There was also a postal service provided for clients who could not attend even an initial fitting. Upon request, sketches of the latest creations, with fabric and trimming samples, were sent. Again, dummies were created for each lady, for garments to be fitted to and the order was posted upon completion.

Ball Gown of cream tamboured net. The bodice is draped, with a centre panel embroidered in chenille and silver thread, c.1900

As Madame Clapham's reputation grew she was called upon to make the robe and mantle worn by the 8th Viscount Chetwynd for the Coronation of George V in 1911. In doing so, Madame Clapham apparently undercut the prices of London tailors considerably. The salon also received many orders for dresses suitable for presentation at court, resulting in Madame Clapham styling herself as Court Dressmaker from 1901. Sets of white gowns were created to be worn at Queen Charlotte's Ball and other important occasions in a young girl's 'coming out' season. One seventeen year old girl recorded her visit to Madame Clapham's to select her gown in 1909, "Today I went with mamma to Hull for the day to get a coming-out frock!! Oh joy, oh joy!! Girls brought in soft piles of silk and satin to exhibit to me. The satin frock has a very simple body draped with gold embroidery with a band of lace across the front. The waist was high and the skirt draped most fascinatingly in panniers, the draperies tied down at the hem in a soft sash-like knot. We decided on this, carried out in white satin, with silver instead of gold. It ought to be perfectly lovely we think!" (3)

Within a few years of establishing herself as a dressmaker in a northern town, Madame Clapham's reputation rose to such heights that gowns created at Kingston Square were considered to be 'good enough' for London and were worn by leading society ladies. Paris would eventually lure ladies who could afford such prices away, but "at present Hull was the rage". (4)

NOTES

(1) The Hull Lady No.5 April 1902, p.24

(2) The Hull Lady December 1901

(3) Extract from a diary belonging to the daughter of a Yorkshire vicar, 1909. Information gathered in the 1970s by Ann Crowther

(4) Left Hand, Right Hand, Sir Osbert Sitwell, Macmillan, 1947, p.224

Day dress of bottle green velvet and ivory silk brocade, 1891. Worn by the wife of Robert Jameson, Mayor of Hull 1870-73, to the wedding of her son, F.W. Jameson to E.M.M. Ayre.

Muriel Wilson, 1895, by Sir William Blake Richmond
Oil on Canvas, Ferens Art Gallery.

Chapter Three - Famous Clientele

As a provincial dressmaker, Madame Clapham's unique success lay in her ability to attract high society clientele, expanding beyond the East Riding. Without formally advertising, the salon relied heavily upon favourable recommendations. Much of Madame Clapham's early and continued success came through the patronage of Miss Muriel Wilson of Tranby Croft, a country house near Hull. Muriel, the daughter of Arthur Wilson, from Hull's famous shipping family, was a renowned Edwardian beauty and a leader of local fashion. Her strong personality and stylish taste in clothes also attracted attention further afield. This is documented in Sir Osbert Sitwell's autobiography, "From the present distance in time it would seem improbable that any fashionable woman should go especially to Hull for her clothes; but so it was. The mode had originated with the daughters of Mrs Arthur Wilson and Mrs Charles Wilson - afterwards Lady Nunburnholme - who, coming from that district, had startled London a few years before with their good looks and their dashing clothes, and had soon made the reputation of the local dressmaker whom they were said to patronise." (1) Muriel Wilson continued to purchase Clapham creations, including her bridal dress and the two bridesmaids gowns for her wedding in 1917. The bridesmaids wore pink pleated georgette dresses, with sleeveless coats of deep cream lace. The bridal outfit was of cream georgette over crepe de chine, with a low neckline, cut square. The distinctive feature was beautiful old rose point lace which formed the front and the square train. (2)

Clients subsequently attracted to the Clapham label included Lady Duff Cooper, the Duchess of Norfolk and Baroness Beaumont. The Museum collection has a beautiful bottle green velvet dress with ivory silk brocade worn by Mrs Robert Jameson, a local figure, to her son's wedding in 1891. Sir Osbert Sitwell recalls his mother owning Clapham gowns. In describing the sitting for the famous family portrait by Sargent in 1900 he states, "The dress worn by mother, though perhaps oddly chosen, was certainly very pretty in its way and had been made by the then celebrated dressmaker, Madame Clapham. I remember accompanying my mother and her cousin, Lady Westmoreland, by train from Scarborough to Hull and then being taken to see Madame Clapham, who was fitting them for the dresses they had ordered for a Court Ball." (3) Lady Ida Sitwell and other society ladies ordered costume from Madame Clapham to wear in a tableaux to be presented at a charity event at the Londesborough Theatre, Scarborough, in aid of the wives and men in South Africa. A tableaux, a 'living picture', was often a representation of a famous painting, acted out yet lasting only a few seconds, the skill being that the 'actors' did not move a muscle. On this particular occasion, the tableaux was a representation of Tennyson's Elaine, with "a pure white robe of crepe-de-chine to be worn by the Countess of Londesborough". As Queen, Lady Ida Sitwell was to wear "a truly regal crown of gold scintillating with jewels, and a quaint flat girdle, stiff with coloured stones." On the evening the theatre was "filled to overflowing with leading County Society". (4) For such a brief moment, the ladies had requested impressive costumes, a show of Edwardian extravagance.

Above Illustration,
Muriel Wilson by Sir J. Sargent Ferens Art Gallery

Madame Clapham was always keen to attract new clientele, through word of mouth or discreet enquiries. One of Madame's workers, Phyllis Thompson, recalls being interviewed for the job in 1926 because she lived near to the Sykes family, "You didn't normally meet Madame Clapham but with mother taking me, she knew we came from Westella and she was very interested in getting hold of Mrs Sykes of Westella Hall, you know, sort of get a few hints how to get in touch." Madame Clapham took pride, however, in the custom she attracted, shown in a rare interview to The Hull Lady in 1901, "To give you some idea as to the large connection I have, I may tell you I make dresses for most of the county and leading society ladies, also a great many for royalty, and I send dresses out to ladies living abroad whom I have never seen." (5) When orders were taken for important clients, employees often worked longer hours to ensure pleasing the ladies.

Madame Clapham's most famous client was Queen Maud of Norway, daughter of Edward VII of England. Whilst never a leader of fashion, Queen Maud, with an admired eighteen inch waist, was stylish. During one of Madame's visits to London she was summoned by telegram to Appleton House at Sandringham and requested to show a selection of model gowns to the Queen. Visits to Sandringham were repeated, with Madame's mannequins, twice a year, as Queen Maud never visited Hull.

The outfits were not personally fitted. The Queen's measurements were recorded and outfits were sewn in Hull. On some occasions employees with slim figures would have outfits fitted against them. Mabel Nutbrown was one of these girls, "I would have to go to the sitting room and have them on there because I was so slim". The Queen's own trimmings of lace or fur were often additional features. A surviving example, a silk blouse, is trimmed with fur around the collar and cuffs. (6) Whilst Queen Maud also acquired outfits from famous London and Paris fashion houses, Clapham creations were worn to various official functions. As these examples show, references appear in her personal dressers' notes between 1919 and 1933. (7)

The Wedding of F. W. Jameson of Eastella to E.M.M. Ayre, 1891. Mrs Robert Jameson, wearing a Clapham creation is seated front row, third from right

MAY 8, 1919 HORSESHOW
khaki - black braid Clapham costume, brown coat, white collar, blue raffia hat
21 OCTOBER 1921 - SANDRINGHAM, DINNER AT H.C. THE KING
blue Clapham dress sequin butterflies, blue wreath
DURING VISIT FROM H.M. QUEEN WILHELMINA
small dinner: Queen Mary's small tiara pearls, Clapham altered sequin dress
1924 - KRISTIANIA (Now known as Oslo) **DINNER**
black morocain, gold embroidered panel dress Clapham; long diamond chain, diamond tiara
1924 - LEGATION BALL
orange embroidered Clapham dress, silver shoes, silver coat; smallest tiara, pearls
26 NOVEMBER 1932 - HER MAJESTY'S BIRTHDAY
Clapham green lace dress
1933 - LUNCH ON BOARD H.M.S NELSON
Clapham spotted blue dress

It was with pride that the salon displayed the mark of royalty, adding further claims of exclusivity and prestige to the name of Madame Clapham.

NOTES
(1) Left Hand, Right Hand, Sir Osbert Sitwell, Macmillan, 1947, p.224
(2) Hull Daily Mail, 1 September 1917, p.4, col.b
(3) Left Hand, Right Hand, Sir Osbert Sitwell, Macmillan, 1947, p.224
(4) The Hull Lady, December 1901; Eastern Morning News, 4 December 1901, p.3
(5) The Hull Lady, December 1901
(6) The blouse is in the Royal Dress Collection, Kunstindustrimuseet, Oslo, Norway.
(7) The diary entries of the Queen's personal maid, Miss Cooper, were passed to Hull Museums in the 1970s to use in the Madame Clapham publication, by the Kunstindustrimuseet, Oslo, Norway.

Chapter Four - The Decline of a Dressmaker

The start of the First World War had a dramatic impact on Madame Clapham's business as society ladies were swapping tea gowns in favour of voluntary service uniforms, resulting in a decline in demand for the exquisite dresses that she produced. Attitudes and social codes changed after the war with women gaining the vote. There was a greater degree of freedom and emancipation for young women from the former restrictions of dress and society. Many of the extravagant feminine designs of Madame Clapham were dropped by the emerging young women of the 1920s who adopted the new shorter, straighter and more decadent styles of the period. The new 1920s look required less material as the younger generation abandoned layers of lining, great trains, and elaborate bodices for a much more flowing, freer and delicate style.

During the 1920s and 1930s the business declined, although Madame Clapham was still sought after by her older pre-war clients and sometimes their unwilling young daughters. The scope of the business also narrowed and became more parochial as many of her London clients looked directly to Paris for their latest fashions and designs. Emily's seasonal visits to York, Harrogate, Grimsby and London ended during this period. One of Madame Clapham's dressmakers remembers the period when the business declined due to greater competition, "Old Madame's name dropped over the years, all these new places opened and you could get all sorts of clothes and clothes changed so much, to ready made things. There was Thorntons, you could go in there and get things. In my day there were only the wealthy people went to Claphams." (Phyllis Thompson, employee 1926-1967) In the 1920s the fall off in custom was demonstrated by the practice of the salon suddenly closing early at 4.30pm, or mid-day during particularly slack seasons of the year. Employees could then be sent home early without notice. During very slack periods some employees were laid off for a month or more.

In order to provide a different line and create interest in her business, Madame Clapham decided to expand into corsetry and provide a service of foundation garments to fit under certain dresses. Her niece Miss Emily MacVitie certainly gained training in this area and possessed a certificate from Gossards of London. In the 1930s Madame Clapham also started to sell a select number of ready-to-wear suits and dress and coat outfits from some of the London fashion salons, although her evening wear remained tailored and exclusive. Whilst attending a Christian Scientist Convention in Chicago in 1931 with her husband Haigh, Emily fell and broke her hip which was a great blow to a lady now in her 70s. As the years wore on, Madame Clapham spent less time at the salon and more time at her home in Cottingham, although she continued to take an interest in the business, receiving regular updates. Emily Wall's son, Eric, remembers Madame Clapham in the 1940s, "We went on holiday to Southport. I remember our suddenly coming across an old woman, Aunt Emmy, in a wheelchair in the main arcade. She was Madame Clapham. I felt I had to be on my best behaviour, stand still and be quiet, whilst the adults talked. I was bored. Madame Clapham had companions and seemed an important person."

The Second World War had an even bigger impact on the Clapham business and almost caused the salon to close. As rationing made fabrics expensive and scarce, many of her employees were made redundant. Many employees were also recruited into the war effort, either in munitions, the services or working on the land. Madame Clapham's clients supported the war time ethos of 'Make do and Mend' as much as possible and so demand for extravagant or lavish clothing severely declined. During the war models were shown locally and were not taken out of the City as they had previously been. However, the salon did manage to keep going during the war without closing and in 1945 business picked up despite the fact that rationing on clothing continued until 1949. Her business relied very heavily on one off single orders for special occasions rather than year round orders from established clients. There was still a demand from her now stalwart elderly clients for gowns for society balls, dances and the races, but these increasingly became off the peg designs from London rather than original made-to-measure outfits.

Kingston Square, c.1885 by F.S. Smith

PRIMITI
METHOD
F.S. Smith

Madame Clapham employees, 1908

Emily Wall and employees, post 1952

Chapter Five - Behind the Scenes

Madame Clapham's clientele seldom caught a glimpse behind the scenes of her Kingston Square salon, but it was here in the workrooms that the intense activity took place which helped to earn her the reputation as a leading dressmaker. Although the workrooms were sparse and cold in appearance, the quality of work produced here required the same high standards and attention to detail which were exhibited in the showroom. The number of girls employed varied, peaking during the heyday to approximately one hundred and fifty and were accommodated in a number of rooms including the bodice room and the skirt room.

Each workroom had a fitter who supervised the work produced and who was responsible for cutting the fabric and ensuring the correct fittings were made for each client. Madame Clapham trained a number of apprentices each year and those lucky enough to be selected stayed on as dressmakers in one of the various workrooms whether it be the skirt, bodice or sleeve room. Apprentices were usually given very basic tasks initially, like picking up pins from the floors and filling up the pin cushions, or making 'strap-holders' for the shoulder bands of evening dresses. They were also required to run errands, particularly fetching supplies from the stockroom or snacks from local outlets. They were supervised in their work by an experienced seamstress. Apprentices were usually based in one room. It was previously believed that girls were kept in one area to maintain secrecy, preventing girls from becoming accomplished in all aspects of dressmaking. In striving for quality and expertise however, perfecting skills in particular areas was probably the best method. Previous employees have said that if they were needed in other areas during busy periods they would be moved, so it was possible to gain a grounding in all aspects of the dressmaking trade. They also had the ability to make complete outfits for themselves and for friends and family outside of work.

Apprentices were selected from a variety of different backgrounds and areas in Hull, "We did a seven year apprenticeship and we started at half past eight in the morning until one or two o'clock and then left at six. No tea break or coffee break. If you were a minute late going in you lost a quarter of an hour. You had a ticket to put in a box. You had to have a medical before you started. After you had done seven years it was really traumatic because they usually used to sack people and you would sit in fear and trembling for the whistle to blow and you would have to go upstairs. But I was one of the lucky ones." (Mabel Nutbrown, former apprentice 1929-1940)

In the early days it seems that the apprentices did not receive a wage for the first year, so it generally attracted girls from families that could afford to support them. This did change in later years as Mabel Nutbrown recalls, "Our full wage after seven years was one pound and ten shillings three ha'penths. You started at five shillings and ninepence and then you got two years at eleven and sixpence, two years at fifteen and threepence. Money didn't seem to come into it in those days you were just glad to have a job, cause I left school at fourteen of course in the holiday time and I started work in September." (Mabel Nutbrown). Although the quality of the training the apprentices received was high and there was a certain prestige attached to being a Clapham 'girl', the pay for workroom girls was low. Many went on to work for other outlets such as Teddy Mintz and Thornton-Varley or they left when they married.

Original working hours were half past eight in the morning until six o'clock in the evening, and until one o'clock in the afternoon on Saturdays. From the 1920s, when the business began to decline, it was not unusual during very quiet periods for girls to work 'three-quarter time', leaving at half past four, or 'half-time', finishing at mid-day. It was even possible for girls to be laid off for periods of time. For time keeping each employee had a brass ticket with a number on it. Each morning it had to be placed in a box near the work entrance, to be collected by a senior member of staff or by Haigh Clapham at quarter to nine and nine o'clock. Girls would lose part of their wages if they arrived later than half past eight. Phyllis Thompson, employee from 1926 until 1967, remembers, "if you was after half past eight you used to lose

Wedding Dress of cream corded silk, c. 1892

quarter of an hour on your wages so dear Miss Holland, when she took the box she used to dawdle a bit, but if Madame's husband, if he came down, he was always dead on time." Legislation for working conditions at one time allowed Madame Clapham to call three notice nights each week, when girls had to work overtime without pay to complete important urgent orders, usually for weddings or funerals. Factory Acts pre-dating 1926 did not permit girls aged sixteen to work overtime, and for girls under the age of eighteen to work later than nine o'clock. It is believed that these rulings were not followed in Madame Clapham's salon. When factory inspectors arrived, the message was passed through the system of speaking tubes linked to all the workrooms, with young girls 'lost' in the wardrobes.

Behind the scenes at Kingston Square the sparse furnishings of the workrooms contrasted dramatically with the plushness and extravagance of the showrooms which Madame Clapham's select clients saw, "My first visits to Aunt Elsie in Kingston Square in Hull were in the 1930s. She did the books for my great Aunt Emmie in a shabby little office at the back of one of the three imposing town houses. The office was on the first floor overlooking run-down Charles Street premises. Elsie Sutcliffe went into the dressmaking business as a 'Hand' in 1896 when she was a girl of eighteen. The dressmaking business was also a refuge for my great Aunt Kate, the widow of Haighs' brother Walter. Kate was housekeeper for Haigh and Emmie and the resident 'Hands' in Kingston Square. I remember the staff basement dining room with its long table. On the upper floors were the sparsely furnished bedrooms with iron beds and the vast old fashioned bathroom. My sister remembers enjoying a meal with the 'hands' in the basement dining room. Haigh and Emmie's dining room was on the ground floor to the left of the front entrance of one of the three houses which was reached by a flight of stone steps from the street. Their meals came up from a hatch in the basement. Towards the back of the ground floor were the showrooms and fitting rooms for receiving wealthy customers." (Pat Walker, great niece of Madame Clapham).

The furnishings for the workrooms were basic. Phyllis Thompson recalls that, "they were very cold and draughty and we had long wooden tables. You used to have a clean sheet over your tables and at night when you went home you put these sheets back over so all your things were kept clean." A central table dominated the room, with the girls seated round it on stools and the floorboards were bare. Most of the work was done by hand. Some of the garments were pressed with heavy flat irons or 'gooses' , "A goose was used in the coat room, the dressmakers didn't use it, it was only the coat hands, they were too heavy for dresses, we just had small irons you know, they were on the gas all day on a low gas. On the landing there was a bucket of water with a hook and you lifted it up and dipped it in, if you had to cool it off." (Mabel Nutbrown) Pleated skirts and intricate garments took a long time to press with the old flat irons. Even in the later years Eric Wall remembers flat irons which you heated by gas and treadle sewing machines still in use at Claphams.

There was an embroidery room based on the top floor. Work was done on frames, using beautiful threads, chenille, pearls, rhinestones and sequins. Intricate designs were placed on to tissue paper, with the pattern sewn on to the fabric through the tissue. At the end the tissue paper had to be picked away. During busy periods it was not unknown for Madame Clapham to send out work to other businesses in Hull. Frances Gray, who worked for Ethel Shields Art Embroidery on Beverley Road, recalls working on outfits and how complicated but enjoyable the work was,"She would send you perhaps a back of a dress and a front and you got on with that and then she would send you the sleeves. Well it wasn't just a little bit of embroidery, it was nearly covered all over and another thing you couldn't transfer them, your transfer had to be sewn on. Mostly beadwork and big sprays all covered in beads and sometimes it was just ordinary embroidery and silk. We did quite a bit for her and I enjoyed the work, but it was all go, you only perhaps had a day and a half to get everything done and finished ready for her to make up."

Madame Clapham ran a disciplined salon, with her workers carrying out her strict orders in the workrooms without question. Girls were not encouraged to talk whilst working and they did not receive regular refreshment breaks, except for lunchtime. Emily Clapham had very little direct contact with the apprentices or 'hands' as they were called, very rarely passing near the workrooms. Mabel Nutbrown remembers her as being "a very hard task master ", assisted in running the place by Miss Borrell and Mrs McKenzie and two mannequinns. Mabel also remembers the only time she saw Madame Clapham, "I did get the sack once. You didn't get holidays, you were stood off and when you were stood off you had to pass your work on to someone else. I was helping Miss Young and someone passed their work on to her and she hadn't got the details. But they came down to the tradesman's entrance and I was standing there talking to these girls asking questions when suddenly they disappeared and this lady came down the stairs in black and she said "what are you doing?" She sacked me on the spot for being down there. However it was sorted out and I was reinstated."

The girls took great pride in their work particularly when orders came in for important clients, such as Queen Maud of Norway, "To me it was a wonderful experience because the materials you used were absolutely out of this world and when the dresses were presented at Court it was wonderful." (Mabel Nutbrown) The beauty of the fabrics used by Madame

Clapham was also impressed upon Phyllis Thompson, "they were all wonderful tweeds and marvellous silks, georgette, there were lots of georgette, I don't suppose you ever see it now." Whilst a hierarchy was in place in the workrooms, from the fitters down to the apprentices, a sense of teamwork did exist. The experienced seamstresses received the most important work, yet most girls who have spoken about their years working for Madame Clapham, remember working on parts of the dresses to be made up for the most important clients. If anyone accidentally dropped blood from a pricked finger onto the fabric, all the girls in the workroom would stop working, chewing pieces of cotton to turn it into a pulp, to dab and absorb the blood from the garment. Workroom girls also socialised together, although usually it was girls from a particular room going out in a group, rather than all the rooms mixing. Trips out to the Saturday matinees were popular, as was the annual trip to Hull Fair. In 1908 twelve girls based in the bodice room were all courting. They agreed that the first to be married would receive a silk blouse and camisole, made by her colleagues in the evenings, as part of her 'trousseau'. Despite the strict working conditions in place at Kingston Square, there were opportunities for camaraderie and humour. When making gowns for larger figures, the girls would joke, "Once around the waist, twice around Hyde Park!" Heyday girls recalled the rhyme about tacking,

"Tack with blue, sure to rue!
Tack with green, not fit to be seen!
Leave in a tack, sure to come back!"

Mabel Nutbrown remembers a particular practical joke, "One day my boss said 'Will you go up to the stockroom and ask for the longstand.' I thought it was strange but I went and Miss Holland was there and I said 'I've come for the longstand' and she said 'stand there and I won't be a minute'. I was stood for ages and I said, 'Miss Holland, are you going to give me that stand?' And then she suddenly said, 'you've stood long enough, you can go now.'" Inevitably, superstitions abounded around the workrooms. Scissors falling to the ground pointing downwards indicated a funeral, whilst a garment dropping to the ground was a sign that it would receive approval from the client. When the girls in the skirt room made a wedding dress they would sew a strand of their hair into the hem as it was considered to bring good luck.

As a strict employer the high standards Madame Clapham imposed upon the workrooms, were crucial to running such a successful business for sixty-five years. In return, however, the girls took pride in their work and received a thorough training, achieving high standards in sewing and embroidery. Kathleen Gardner, whose sister, Evelyn, was an apprentice from 1911-1915, recognised this, "There was no doubt it was very fastiduous work of the highest quality and although my mother had always been a very keen seamstress all her life, she must have learnt a great deal from the very precise work and way of doing things. It was very useful for me being younger, because as I grew up she always taught me the correct way of doing any sewing, as the perfectionist that Madame Clapham had turned out."

By Appointment to The Late Queen Maud of Norway

Telephone 34147

Kingston Square,
Hull, ______________ 19___

M______________________________

Bought of Madame Clapham,

Court Dressmaker

Terms:
Cash without discount

5% Interest charged on all Overdue Accounts.

Evening dress with matching bolero, of indigo chiffon with stylised floral print, c.1929

French Edwardian designs purchased by Madame Clapham

One of Madame Clapham's models who would have worked in the showrooms. Date unknown

Employees of Madame Clapham on a day out. Date unknown

Chapter Six - The Showroom and Models

From the early days, even when Madame Clapham operated on a small scale, the showroom was designed to exude elegance and exclusivity. To attract the leading county families, Madame Clapham recognised the need to create the right atmosphere and environment which would impress and tempt the ladies. The showroom was a long wide room, painted white and grey, with beautifully thick carpets and comfortable sofas. The bay windows were adorned with rose-coloured draped curtains. Eric Wall, nephew of Madame Clapham, recalls from his youth that the showroom stretched across the back of numbers 1 and 2 Kingston Square, with an archway into number 3. An additional showroom reached along John Street, with large windows on either side. The room was also furnished with small displays of garments, examples of day wear, evening gowns and lingerie. These displays were beautifully arranged and were attended to by the models or mannequins. They often left an impression upon visitors to the salon. A young girl visiting in 1909 recorded in her diary of "folds of silk and net, of pale cloth and velvet, embroideries of pearl and silver and dull gold and lace, petticoats with pleated frills, lacy blouses." (1) Desks were provided for staff, including one for the secretary and one for Millicent Clapham, who made sketches of gowns. There was also a large desk, decorated with the fleur de lis, at which Eric Wall recalls seeing Uncle Haigh sitting, looking over the accounts. This was also where cash, cheque books and headed notepaper were kept.

The fitting rooms, three in total, were designed to offer space and comfort. The mirrors were arranged to allow clients to view themselves in their Clapham creation from all sides. To allow this, the mirrors were fitted on hinges, as Eric Wall recalls, "taking great pleasure in the sound of the way the front glass panels ran smoothly on ball bearings when you moved them along their length. Multicoloured sumptuous dresses were shown off to good effect on this. I particularly remember being impressed by a dress with a design of liquorice allsorts all over it!" One room, which caught the sun through one of the bay windows, was used for the fitting of day dresses, morning and afternoon wear. A second room was designed for the fitting of evening wear, particularly ball gowns, with shutters placed upon the windows. The room was lit by gas lamps, later electric lighting, to create the right effect for when the gown would be viewed in public. For final fittings ladies were encouraged to add their chosen accessories to create the full effect. This is an excellent example of Madame Clapham's attention to detail and desire for exclusivity.

The mannequins, dressed in black, worked entirely in the showroom. They were primarily chosen for their good looks and slim figures. They were well-groomed, graceful and polite to attend to the important clients who visited the showroom. Their main responsibilities were to model gowns for clients, arrange and attend to displays and to pack the garments. Dresses were packed using layers and layers of tissue paper. One girl later went to work at Thornton-Varley's store and was told she used too many layers. During busy periods, the mannequins would also work overtime, ready to pack completed gowns and deliver them to the post office or the railway station. Unlike the workroom girls, they came into contact with Madame's clients and, during the heyday in particular, they came into contact with Madame Clapham herself when she often supervised fittings. When Madame Clapham was in the showroom, the models could neither sit down nor speak. She was said to have had a temper which was expressed on occasions. One account describes how the head dressmaker had spent hours pinning up material for a dress on a model, only to have it pulled to pieces by Madame Clapham, reducing the girl to tears. Another recollection, however, shows kindness towards one girl who worked in the showroom. When she was sick, Madame Clapham visited her with a gift of pink carnations.

The models and the workroom girls did not mix at the salon but nor did they socially. The luxurious setting of the showroom probably appeared to be worlds apart from the sparse furnishings and working conditions in the sewing rooms. Although apprentices were sent into the showroom to pick up pins from the floor, this was usually after the salon had closed for business. Only the fitters were allowed to attend to ladies for the fitting of outfits. Communication was maintained between the showroom and the workrooms through speaking tubes. This exclusivity seems to have broken down in later years. Phyllis Thompson, employed at Clapham's from 1926 until 1967, was from the start based in the workrooms, but under Emily Wall she was allowed into the showroom and was able to communicate with customers. Mrs Wall noticed Phyllis's skill in assisting ladies in selecting an outfit and leaving the salon satisfied. Phyllis recalls that the chosen garment was often not the same as the one they had originally been fitted in, "I would go in and fish something out which suited them a lot nicer and half the time wasn't so expensive, because if you've got a happy customer she'll come back, but a woman goes and spends a lot of money on something and probably never wears it, it always rankles with her, they never forget."

Madame Clapham's outfits were expensive and exclusive, although the subject of money was only discussed discreetly, if at all, at the salon, for fear of sounding 'vulgar'. More often than not the bill for a particular gown or coat was sent directly to the lady's husband without mentioning the cost to the customer herself. To create an impression of costs, in 1916 a dress suitable to wear to a wedding was priced at 7 guineas, in comparison to a train fare from York to Hull in the same year costing 2/6d and a three course lunch priced at 3/-. In 1926 a blue georgette evening dress cost 8 guineas and a green chiffon gown with embossed velvet cost 10 guineas. A 1948 wedding dress of moire silk was made for 38 guineas and in 1951 a blue taffeta evening dress with matching overskirt cost £25. The accounts were made up in the showroom, calculating the fabric and trimmings used, from records kept as the garments were made. One previous employee from the heyday claimed that a further £10 was then added to the cost. The price of Madame Clapham's outfits reflected the exclusivity of the gowns and the quality of the fabric and needlework. Inevitably, the growth of ready-to-wear clothing increasingly available from Hull stores such as Thornton-Varley's created greater competition than the salon could eventually cope with, and the steady decline could not be averted without changing the whole ethos of Madame Clapham's business.

NOTES

(1) Extract from the diary of a Yorkshire vicar's daughter, 1909. Information gathered in the 1970s by Ann Crowther

Emily and Haigh Clapham in their later years.

Chapter Seven - The End of an Era

When Madame Clapham died on the 10th January 1952 at the age of ninety six, it was almost as if a legend in Hull had died. Eric Wall remembers the moment, "I was thirteen at the time and away at school. In our family the adults never talked about their age because to do so was contrary to Christian Science teachings. Aunt Emmy strongly believed in this and I think she and Uncle Haigh visited Christian Science's mother church in Boston, USA. She also gave money to the First Church of Christ Scientists on Beverley Road and may have been its principle benefactor. I had no idea at the time that she was so old."

Following Madame Clapham's death, number 2 Kingston Square was closed down and sold at auction. With the legacy that Emily Wall received from Madame Clapham, she purchased number 3, which was larger and continued the business under her aunt's name. Eric Wall commented that his mother, "felt able thereby to continue to call Madame Clapham's 'Court Dressmaker'. I felt a bit uncomfortable about this as I certainly didn't see any royalty." Emily Wall was, however, still able to attract local and regional 'society' ladies to the salon because she acquired the latest London designs at the beginning of every season. The Walls lived on the first floor and the salons were situated on the ground floor. Eric Wall has memories from these years, "Trade slipped more and more away as the range of choice in popular shops extended and fine hand workmanship was not needed. Some of the girls were particularly valued by my mother. I remember her speaking highly of a Miss Whitely [the rugby player, Johnny Whitely's sister]. I also remember another woman, Miss Barrett, who was not called a 'girl' because she worked in the showrooms and sometimes modelled the clothes."

Emily Wall had started as a live-in apprentice and worked her way up through the ranks. Over the years she gradually became more fatigued and suffered from swollen ankles. She, like Madame Clapham, worked hard and did not give in easily to illness. Emily Wall is described by her son Eric, "My mother had a stoicism which she learnt from Aunt Emmy as well as her Christian Science. Favourite axioms of hers, were, as to be expected 'a stitch in time saves nine', 'procrastination is the thief of time' and 'if at first you don't succeed try, try again'. She died in harness. Despite her swollen legs and heart disease she refused to sit down whilst local trawler owners and landed gentry 'interminably' tried on the latest haute couture. After all she had been trained that way by her Aunt. "

Madame Clapham's death heralded the end of an era of elegant and exclusive fashion in the region. Although the salon and to a certain extent, her ethos and standards, continued until the death of her niece, Emily Wall, in 1967, the business was gradually declining. With sixty five years of high class dressmaking, Madame Clapham was unique in the sense that she earned royal patronage through Queen Maud of Norway, a particular achievement for a provincial business woman from Hull. Despite her strictness in the salon, Madame Clapham was held in high esteem by her clients and employees for the quality and individuality of the fashions she produced. Although many of her workers rarely saw her in their day-to-day work, she left a strong impression on them all through the way she ran her business, the high standards she demanded of them and her striving for exclusiveness and excellence. Employees had a strong sense of pride in the work they produced and enjoyed nothing better than hearing of the society balls in which their work was shown off. Their pride was heightened by an awareness of the superiority of Madame Clapham's high quality garments in comparison with the products of the rival dressmaking businesses in Hull. The height of Madame Clapham's popularity and standing as a royal and court dressmaker has lived on in the memory of her now elderly clients and faithful employees, Mabel Nutbrown remembers, "I can't explain the feeling when you touched the material, it was absolutely wonderful, and when you made a wedding dress, you were really proud of it. It was a wonderful life, I would love to go through it again."

Evening dress of black velvet, with gold lurex and rhinestone decoration, c.1930-32

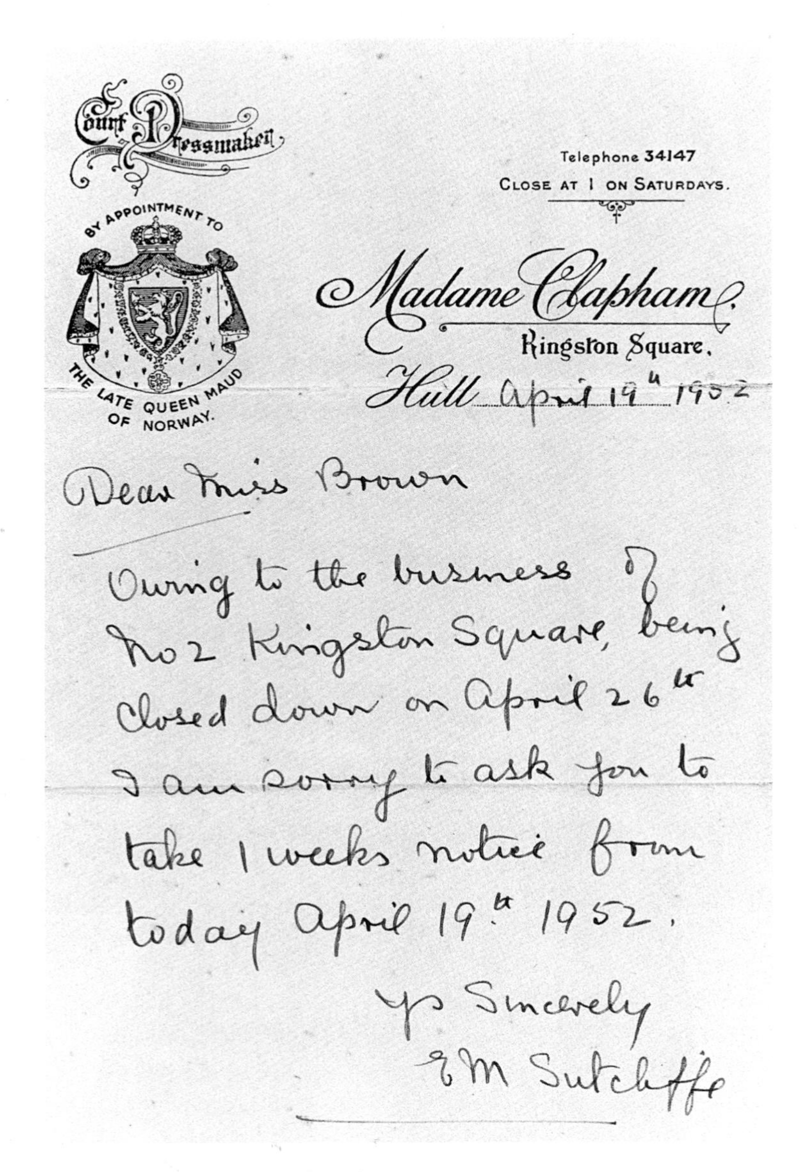

Court Dressmaker

By Appointment to The Late Queen Maud of Norway.

Telephone 34147
Close at 1 on Saturdays.

Madame Clapham
Kingston Square,
Hull April 19th 1952

Dear Miss Brown

Owing to the business of No 2 Kingston Square, being closed down on April 26th I am sorry to ask you to take 1 weeks notice from today April 19th 1952.

Yrs Sincerely
E M Sutcliffe

Letter of dismissal, 1952 following the death of Madame Clapham and the closure of No.2 Kingston Square

Evening dress of black satin crepe and gold lurex, c.1924